Ingredients for a Healthy Life

PERFECT PASTA Recipes

Gareth Stevens
PUBLISHING

By Kristen Rajczak

Please visit our website, www.garethstevens.com. For a free color catalog of all our high-quality books, call toll free 1-800-542-2595 or fax 1-877-542-2596.

Library of Congress Cataloging-in-Publication Data

Rajczak, Kristen.
Perfect pasta recipes / by Kristen Rajczak.
  p. cm. — (Ingredients for a healthy life)
Includes index.
ISBN 978-1-4824-0572-9 (pbk.)
ISBN 978-1-4824-0574-3 (6-pack)
ISBN 978-1-4824-0571-2 (library binding)
1. Cooking (Pasta) — Juvenile literature. 2. Pasta products — Juvenile literature. I. Rajczak, Kristen. II. Title.
TX394.5 R35 2014
641.3—dc23

First Edition

Published in 2015 by
Gareth Stevens Publishing
111 East 14th Street, Suite 349
New York, NY 10003

Copyright © 2015 Gareth Stevens Publishing

Designer: Andrea Davison-Bartolotta
Editor: Kristen Rajczak

Photo credits: Cover, pp. 1, 3, 7, 9, 13, 15, 17, 21–24 (pasta background) Ohn Mar/Shutterstock.com; cover, p. 1 (macaroni and cheese) Maria Komar/Shutterstock.com; cover, p. 1 (orzo) Wiktory/Shutterstock.com; cover, pp. 1 (lasagna), 13 (lasagna), 18, 21 (arrows) iStockphoto/Thinkstock; p. 4 mexrix/Shutterstock.com; p. 5 Pixland/Thinkstock; p. 7 Michele Cozzolino/Shutterstock.com; p. 8 Zerbor/Shutterstock.com; p. 9 (both) courtesy of Andrea Davison-Bartolotta; p. 10 Roberto Mettifogo/Photographer's Choice/Getty Images; p. 11 David Young-Wolff/Photographer's Choice/Getty Images; p. 12 El Nariz/Shutterstock.com; p. 13 (jalapeños) Javier Correa/Shutterstock.com; p. 14 (top) AntonioGravante/Shutterstock.com; p. 14 (bottom) nito/Shutterstock.com; p. 15 Brent Hofacker/Shutterstock.com; p. 16 Jose Luis Stephens/Radius Images/Getty Images; p. 17 (orzo) BW Folsom/Shutterstock.com; p. 17 (broccoli) Reika/Shutterstock.com; p. 17 (asparagus) ksulee/Shutterstock.com; p. 17 (avocado) Hong Vo/Shutterstock.com; p. 17 (cilantro) brulove/Shutterstock.com; p. 19 (top) Daniel Acker/Bloomberg via Getty Images; p. 19 (bottom) PhotoAlto/Laurence Mouton/Getty Images; p. 20 Francesco83/Shutterstock.com; p. 21 (boy) Comstock/Thinkstock.

All rights reserved. No part of this book may be reproduced in any form without permission in writing from the publisher, except by a reviewer.

Printed in the United States of America

CPSIA compliance information: Batch #CS15GS: For further information contact Gareth Stevens, New York, New York at 1-800-542-2595.

Contents

Recipes in this book may use knives, mixers, and hot stove tops. Ask for an adult's help when using these tools.

Words in the glossary appear in **bold** type the first time they are used in the text.

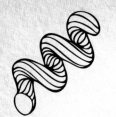

By Any Name

In Poland, there's pierogi (puh-ROH-gee). Germans and Hungarians eat spaetzle (SHPEHT-sluh). Orzo is common in Greece. Even if you've never tried these, you're likely familiar with something similar—pasta!

In the United States, pasta is commonly thought of as Italian **cuisine**. We most often prepare it in the Italian style, boiled in water and served with tomato sauce. But it can be tossed with just about any meat, sauce, and vegetable! The **recipes** in this book are mostly fun, healthy takes on Italian pasta dishes.

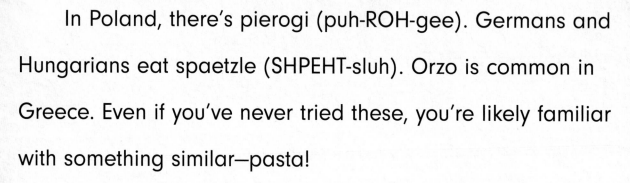

Do You Have Allergies?

The recipes in this book may use **ingredients** that contain or have come into contact with nuts, gluten, dairy products, and other common causes of **allergies**. If you have any food allergies, please ask a parent or teacher for help when cooking and tasting!

Pasta is inexpensive to buy and make. That's one reason it's so popular!

5

A Long Time Coming

Though it's hard to say where pasta was first made, we do know it's been made for thousands of years. Pasta dough is a simple combination of flour and water or eggs. The same ingredients are used to make similar dough in **cultures** around the world!

However, **archaeologists** think central Asia was a likely place for the creation of the first noodles. In the 8th century, the Arab people took over the part of Europe that's now Italy, probably introducing pasta to that area.

CHEW ON THIS!

It wasn't until the mid-1800s that southern Italian cooks began pairing tomatoes and pasta. When tomatoes first arrived from the Americas, Europeans thought they were poisonous. They're nightshades, a plant family that does have some poisonous members!

Supersimple Spaghetti Sauce

makes 6 servings

Ingredients:

1 tablespoon olive oil

1 medium onion, finely chopped

2 cloves garlic, minced

2 (28-ounce) cans whole tomatoes, drained, tomatoes chopped

3 tablespoons tomato paste

1 teaspoon dried oregano

1 bay leaf

Salt and pepper

One of the most popular ways to serve pasta is with tomato sauce! Make an easy, tasty sauce using this recipe. Enjoy it with your favorite pasta.

Directions:

1. Heat olive oil in a large pot on the stove top on medium-low heat. Add the onion and cook for about 5 minutes, stirring it a few times.
2. Mix in the garlic and cook for about 2 minutes.
3. Add the canned tomatoes, tomato paste, oregano, bay leaf, and a pinch of salt and pepper. Cook on low for about 30 minutes, uncovered. The sauce will thicken.
4. If you like a smoother sauce, allow the sauce to cool and use a blender or food processor to break down the tomato chunks.
5. Serve over pasta.

The Italian Takeover

When pasta reached the area around the Mediterranean Sea, durum wheat began to be the major flour used to make pasta, just as it is today. By the 1300s, dried pastas made the Italian way were circling the globe! They lasted a long time before being cooked and so made good stores aboard ships.

Pasta first came to the Americas with Spanish settlers. But it was the arrival of Italian **immigrants** in the late 1800s that truly began the pasta craze in the United States.

CHEW ON THIS!

Thomas Jefferson was a pasta lover! While staying in Paris, France, for a few years in the late 1700s, Jefferson ate macaroni. He liked it so much he brought two cases of it back to the United States when he returned.

Spaghetti Pizza

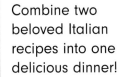

makes about 8 servings

Combine two beloved Italian recipes into one delicious dinner!

Ingredients:

1 (8-ounce) package spaghetti, broken into 2-inch pieces
1 egg
1/4 cup milk
2 cups shredded, low-fat mozzarella cheese
1/4 teaspoon salt
1/4 teaspoon garlic salt
1 (16-ounce) jar spaghetti sauce
1 teaspoon dried oregano
1/4 teaspoon dried basil
pizza toppings (sliced pepperoni, peppers, pineapple, choose your favorite)

Directions:

1. Preheat oven to 425 degrees.
2. Fill a pot with water and bring it to a boil on the stove top. Add the spaghetti and cook for about 10 minutes. Drain the pasta in a **colander**.
3. Beat the egg in a bowl. Mix in milk, 1/2 cup of the mozzarella cheese, salt, and garlic salt. Stir in the spaghetti.
4. Prepare a baking dish with cooking spray. Spread the spaghetti mixture evenly in the bottom. This will be the "crust."
5. Bake for 15 minutes.
6. Take the "crust" out of the oven, and reduce the oven temperature to 350 degrees.
7. Spread sauce on the crust. Add the rest of the cheese and sprinkle with the oregano and basil. Top with your favorite pizza toppings.
8. Bake for 30 minutes. Allow the pizza to cool for 5 minutes before cutting.

9

How It's Made

Dried pasta is a quick and easy way to enjoy a delicious meal. Some people still make it by hand, though.

First, semolina—the flour made from durum wheat—is carefully mixed with warm water or eggs. It's **kneaded** for several minutes and left to rest. Next, the dough is rolled out and put through a pasta machine, which stretches the dough to the needed thickness. The pasta is then cut into ribbons or shapes and cooked or frozen.

durum wheat field

CHEW ON THIS!

Pasta made in a factory is made in much the same way as homemade pasta, just on a larger scale. In addition, shapes—such as the popular elbow macaroni—can be made using molds and sheets with holes in them.

It takes extra time to make homemade pasta, but the taste is worth it!

11

The Shape of a Meal

Spaghetti and tomato sauce seem perfect together. Here are a few other pastas with tips on how to serve them.

- angel hair: Sometimes called capellini, angel hair pasta is very thin, so it goes best with light or creamy sauces.

- manicotti: Shaped like long, wide tubes, manicotti noodles are stuffed with cheese and meat, and baked.

- ravioli and tortellini: These stuffed pastas may hold meat, **pureed** (pyuh-RAYD) vegetables, or cheese. They can be cooked in soups, served with tomato sauce, or just tossed with a little garlic and olive oil.

CHEW ON THIS!

Fettuccine is another popular pasta. It's egg pasta that looks like thicker, flat spaghetti. Fettuccine is often served with cream sauces.

fettuccine alfredo

Mexican Lasagna

makes 4 servings

Ingredients:

3/4 cup salsa from a jar

1 1/2 teaspoons cumin

1 (14.5-ounce) can no-salt-added diced tomatoes

1 (8-ounce) can no-salt-added tomato sauce

6 precooked lasagna noodles

1 cup frozen whole-kernel corn, thawed

1 (15-ounce) can black beans, rinsed and drained

2 cups shredded, low-fat Mexican-blend cheese

1/4 cup chopped green onions

Black beans and salsa add a healthy, yummy twist to everyday lasagna recipes. Do you like spicy food? Use a hotter salsa, or add some jalapeños to the top!

jalapeños

Directions:

1. Preheat oven to 450 degrees.
2. Mix together salsa, cumin, diced tomatoes, and tomato sauce. Spray a small, square baking dish with cooking spray, and spread about 2/3 cup of the sauce in the bottom.
3. Place two of the noodles over the sauce.
4. Top the noodles with about 1/2 cup each of the corn and beans. Sprinkle with about 1/2 cup of cheese, followed by another 2/3 cup of sauce.
5. Make another layer in the same way.
6. Top with the last two noodles. Cover the noodles with the remaining sauce, then the rest of the cheese.
7. Cover with tin foil. Bake for about 30 minutes.
8. Before serving, sprinkle the onions on top.

Good for You

Pasta can be a great part of a balanced **diet**. It's a good source of some **nutrients**, including vitamin A, which helps keep your eyes, skin, and bones healthy. Pasta also provides carbohydrates, the main nutrient your body uses for energy.

Whole-wheat pasta is an even better choice for your body! It has fiber and protein. They aren't found in great amounts in traditional pastas because the parts of wheat that have these nutrients are removed before the flour is ground.

CHEW ON THIS!

An easy way to introduce your family to whole-wheat pasta is by replacing half of the regular pasta in a recipe with whole-wheat. Slowly increase the amount until all your pasta in a recipe is whole-wheat!

whole-wheat pasta

Easy Macaroni and Cheese

Makes 4 servings

Ingredients:

1 1/4 cups uncooked whole-wheat elbow macaroni
1 cup 1 percent milk
2 tablespoons all-purpose flour
1 1/4 cups shredded, low-fat sharp cheddar cheese
1/2 teaspoon salt
1/8 teaspoon pepper
1 1/4 cups whole-wheat breadcrumbs
1 tablespoon butter, melted

> Lots of vegetables taste great with pasta and cheese. Pump up the healthfulness of this recipe by mixing in some broccoli, peas, or zucchini!

Directions:

1. Cook the macaroni by following the directions on the box. Drain it well.
2. Heat a medium-sized pan on the stove top on medium heat. Mix together milk and flour in the pan for about 2 minutes or until thick.
3. Add cheese, salt, and pepper, stirring with a fork or whisk until smooth.
4. Stir in pasta and coat with the cheese mixture. Turn the heat off, cover, and let stand for 4 minutes.
5. Heat a skillet on the stove top and lightly toast breadcrumbs for about 5 minutes, stirring a few times. Add melted butter and mix together.
6. After about 2 minutes, remove the skillet from heat and sprinkle the breadcrumb and butter mixture over the macaroni. Serve right away.

Portion Trouble

There aren't a lot of health concerns about pasta itself, especially if you choose whole-wheat. The problem lies in how much pasta you eat!

It's hard to figure out the right amount of pasta to put on your plate. Italian restaurants aren't any help—they fill your plate up! When you're at home, give yourself a helping of cooked pasta about the size of your fist. That's one serving. For many people, that ends up being between 3/4 cup and 1 cup of cooked pasta.

CHEW ON THIS!

Pasta is just one part of a balanced meal. If you divide up your plate, about half should be covered in veggies, and the other half divided between the pasta and a protein, such as chicken or fish.

Veggie-Powered Orzo Salad

makes 4 servings

Ingredients:

Salad:

1 cup uncooked whole-wheat orzo

9 asparagus, the woody ends trimmed off and the rest cut into 1-inch pieces

1 head broccoli, cut into small trees

1 handful cilantro, chopped

1 handful alfalfa sprouts

1/3 cup almonds, chopped and toasted

1/2 of a small cucumber, chopped

1 avocado, sliced into small pieces

1/4 cup crumbled feta cheese

Dressing:

1 clove garlic, mashed and minced

1 pinch salt

2 tablespoons fresh lemon juice

1/4 cup extra-virgin olive oil

> Orzo is small pasta that's shaped a lot like rice. This recipe calls for the addition of lots of veggies to give you a big serving without too much pasta!

Directions:

1. Fill a large pot with water and bring it to a boil on the stove top. Add orzo and cook according to the package directions. The pasta should be cooked without being mushy.
2. Just before the orzo is done, stir the asparagus and broccoli into the boiling water. Allow the vegetables to cook for about 30 seconds.
3. Remove the pan from the heat, and pour the pasta and vegetables into a colander to drain. Run cold water over them for about 2 minutes to stop them from cooking more.
4. In a small bowl, combine the garlic, lemon juice, extra-virgin olive oil, and salt. Use a fork to mix together well.
5. Toss the orzo, broccoli, asparagus, and cilantro with about half the dressing.
6. Add the sprouts, almonds, cucumber, avocado, and feta cheese. Toss gently. Serve immediately or refrigerate. Add more dressing as needed.

Many Choices

Today, nontraditional pastas are sold in many grocery stores. You can find pasta made of spelt and buckwheat flours, two tasty grains. But some pastas don't use grains at all. They might use pea or lentil flour instead!

Brown rice and quinoa (KEEN-wah) pastas have become a common choice for people suffering from celiac disease. Their bodies react badly to gluten, a protein found in wheat and some other grains, such as rye and barley. Regular pasta would make them feel quite sick.

CHEW ON THIS!

Gnocchi (NYO-kee) is chewy pasta made from potatoes. Though it's filling and hearty on its own, gnocchi is commonly served with thicker sauces. A little butter can also go a long way on a plate of gnocchi!

gnocchi

These pastas are made for people who follow a certain diet or just want to try something new.

Make It Your Own!

Now that you know all about pasta, get creative in the kitchen! There are so many possibilities.

- Toss rigatoni with some peas and pesto, a sauce made with basil and garlic.

- Serve cold Asian noodles and steamed broccoli with a drizzle of a nutty sauce made by mixing 1/4 cup soy sauce, 1 tablespoon peanut butter, and 1/2 teaspoon ginger.

- Cook up some Polish pierogi in a frying pan with a little butter and a chopped-up onion. Yum!

Making your own pasta is a really fun way to spend an afternoon. Ask an adult to help you find everything you need!

Healthy Reasons to Eat Pasta

Vitamin A keeps skin, bones, and eyes healthy.

Potassium is a nutrient in pasta that helps your heart and muscles work well.

Whole-wheat pasta is a good source of fiber, which helps the body keep food moving.

The protein in whole-wheat pasta helps in muscle growth and repair.

Carbohydrates give you lots of energy to run and play.

Glossary

allergy: a body's sensitivity to usually harmless things in the surroundings, such as dust, pollen, or mold

archaeologist: a scientist who studies ancient buildings and objects to learn about past human life and activities

colander: a bowl with small holes used for washing or draining food

cuisine: a style of cooking

culture: the beliefs and ways of life of a group of people

diet: the food one usually eats

immigrant: one who comes to a new country to settle there

ingredient: a food that is mixed with other foods

knead: to work with dough until it's smooth

nutrient: something a living thing needs to grow and stay alive

puree: to grind or blend cooked food into a thick paste or liquid. Also, the paste or liquid itself.

recipe: an explanation of how to make food

For More Information

BOOKS

Dolbear, Emily J. *How Did That Get to My Table? Pasta.* Ann Arbor, MI: Cherry Lake Publishing, 2010.

Marsico, Katie. *Your Healthy Plate. Grains.* Ann Arbor, MI: Cherry Lake Publishing, 2012.

Rau, Dana M. *Recipes from Italy.* Chicago, IL: Capstone Raintree, 2014.

WEBSITES

How to Make Fresh Pasta
www.chow.com/videos/show/all/54274/how-to-make-fresh-pasta
Watch this video to learn how to make a simple pasta using a pasta machine.

Kids Corner
www.ilovepasta.org/public/kids-corner
Read cool facts about pasta, and find good recipe and craft ideas.

Publisher's note to educators and parents: Our editors have carefully reviewed these websites to ensure that they are suitable for students. Many websites change frequently, however, and we cannot guarantee that a site's future contents will continue to meet our high standards of quality and educational value. Be advised that students should be closely supervised whenever they access the Internet.

Index